Computers
and talking to
People

Andrew Powney

Computers
and talking to
People

A pragmatic guide to stakeholder engagement for IT, technology and digital programmes and projects

Andrew Powney

SIMPLE
TECH
RESULTS

Published by Simple Tech Results Ltd

ISBN: 978-1-7395357-0-4

CONTENTS

AN INVITATION TO CONNECT

This guide is based on my personal experience working collaboratively with many different people. If you want to join in the conversation or you want additional help or training on your programme or project, please feel free to connect with me on LinkedIn or find me at www.simpletechresults.co.uk. There, you will also find large colour versions of the diagrams in the book published for your use under a Creative Commons licence.

ACKNOWLEDGMENTS

Publishing the book would not have been possible without help. Thank you, Shiona Macorkindale, Mike Shannon and Rita Amartey for your help editing, corrections and feedback on the various drafts.

INTRODUCTION

Many programme and project management methods[1] stress the importance of stakeholder engagement but don't advise people how to go about doing it. This guide fills that gap with a process that any project manager, change manager or stakeholder engagement manager can use.

Many people accept the importance of stakeholder engagement theoretically but are unsure how to start, so it may tend to get lost amongst other priorities. In this guide, the three steps to successful stakeholder engagement are: developing your key messages, mapping stakeholders, and engaging with stakeholders. Obviously, the highest priority of these steps is engaging with stakeholders, but the first two steps are essential to do that effectively.

Who is this guide for?

If your challenge is knowing where to start, this guide is for you. If you need clarification about what to say and when this guide is for you. If you worry that stakeholders are too busy, this guide is for you. If you want to get the support of your

[1] Managing Successful Programmes (MSP), Agile Project Management (AgilePM), Prince2 Project Management

programme colleagues, this guide is for you. If you want to write a stakeholder engagement strategy, this guide is for you.

A note on the terminology

This guide covers stakeholder engagement for both programmes and projects. For ease of reading, we use the term 'programmes' to mean programmes and projects throughout this guide. The term 'project' is only used when referencing a project specifically.

Within stakeholder engagement, the terms stakeholder engagement and stakeholder management are often used interchangeably. Most recently the term stakeholder engagement has become favoured and is used in this book. The key reasons for this change centre on the following arguments

- You must engage stakeholders, as you cannot manage people you have no authority over
- Stakeholder management is just old programme management terminology – engagement is what we do now
- Management is about following a process, and engagement is about building relationships

The Association for Project Management (APM) explores this in more detail in the book Engaging Stakeholders on projects: How to harness people power by Elizabeth Harrin[2].

We refer to stakeholder engagement as SE throughout this guide.

---

[2] Harrin, E. (2020) Engaging Stakeholders on projects: How to harness people power. Princes Risborough. Association for Project Management

1

WHY IS STAKEHOLDER ENGAGEMENT IMPORTANT?

It's worth taking a moment to consider why SE is essential for IT, technology and digital programmes. Doing SE takes time and effort, some of that effort could be allocated more directly to delivery. So why should we do it? Understanding this and sharing it can help convince colleagues about the benefits and get their buy-in. The main reasons boil down to achieving better outcomes and managing programme risks.

Achieving better outcomes

Many programme and project management methods regularly used for IT, technology and digital programmes specifically include the topic of SE and identify it as increasingly crucial to successful or better outcomes. Detailed here are some specific examples.

The Managing Successful Programmes (MSP) framework states that 'how a programme engages its stakeholders is crucial to its success' and encourages the development of a specific SE strategy.

The PRINCE2 project management method states, 'effective communication with key stakeholders, both internal and external to the corporate organisation, is essential to the project's success' and articulates how, in part, a project's Communication Management Strategy can be derived from a programme's SE strategy.

AgilePM training and the related DSDM® Agile Project Framework promotes 'a strong focus on communication between and the involvement of all the stakeholders in the system'. SE is an aspect within five of the framework roles, Business Sponsor, Business Visionary, Technical Coordinator, Project Manager, and Business Analyst. People in these roles are expected to ensure appropriate stakeholder involvement in three of the framework's eight principles: focus on the business need, collaborate, and communicate continuously and clearly.

Managing programme risks

Proactively managing risks is an essential strand of programme management. Accepting that many risks are relatively generic across programmes, effective SE will help mitigate the following risks:

- There is a risk that stakeholders will not be interested in the programme. The cause of this is a lack of effective engagement by the programme. The effect of this risk could vary from stakeholders being focused on alternative priorities to actively becoming difficult or obstructive.
- There is a risk that users will continue to develop their own systems and workarounds to meet the same need as the programme. The cause of this is stakeholders not being made aware that, in time, the programme delivery will meet their need. The effect of this risk is unnecessary extra expense and effort incurred by the organisation.

- There is a risk that programme team members will say different things to the same stakeholder. The cause of this is that different people have different levels of knowledge and communication skills. The effect of this is stakeholders having a poor experience and potential loss of confidence in the programme.
- There is a risk that the programme will ask too much of some stakeholders and not enough of others. This causes different people to be drawn to the same helpful stakeholders, unaware of their work for others. The effect of this is some stakeholders not fulfilling their potential.

There is also always a wider programme risk that the programme will fail. There are many reasons it might fail and one of these, that SE can help mitigate, is 'poor stakeholder engagement'. You may have some examples of your own you can refer to. If not, some high-profile examples that I found online include:

The UK NHS National Program for IT was a large-scale IT program in the early 2000s to digitise patient records and improve information sharing across healthcare providers. However, the project faced significant challenges due to a need for more stakeholder engagement. Many healthcare professionals felt excluded from the decision-making process, leading to resistance and concerns about the system's usability and effectiveness. The program was eventually abandoned in 2011 after significant cost overruns and delays.

The Los Angeles Unified School District's iPad Initiative was a programme launched in 2013 to provide iPads to every student and teacher in the district. However, the initiative faced criticism for its lack of stakeholder engagement. Teachers were not adequately involved in the planning and decision-making, resulting in curriculum integration and technical support issues. The program was suspended in 2014 after numerous implementation challenges, including problems with device management and security.

The Queensland Health Payroll System was a programme launched in 2010 by the Queensland Health Department in Australia to implement a new payroll system to manage employee salaries. The project encountered significant difficulties due to a lack of stakeholder engagement, including inadequate testing and insufficient end-user involvement. As a result, the system encountered numerous errors, resulting in thousands of overpayments, underpayments, and delays in employee salary processing. The project became a major controversy and resulted in significant financial losses.

2

STEP 1 – DEVELOPING KEY MESSAGES

Developing key messages is the first step of effective SE. Key messages about your programme are the main points you want to share with your stakeholders. Mostly, they are the important things you want to tell stakeholders, but sometimes they may be about what you need from them, such as their requirements, an org chart, an insight into when best to deploy etc. It's important to note that key messages will develop throughout the programme's lifecycle and don't have to be perfect or all be developed at the start. Still, the better they are, the easier it will be to engage with your stakeholders.

Create once and use many times

Key messages should conform to the mantra 'create once and use many times'. Once developed, they can be used in visual, written, or verbal formats. They can also be used by anyone representing the programme, not just by those who developed them.

Programme name

The number one key message of any programme is its name. It might seem obvious, but it's not unheard of that early on the name of a programme is still undecided. Ideally, the programme name is self-explanatory. For example, 'Google Cloud Print replacement project' is an excellent self-explanatory name that springs to mind. It does what it says on the tin. One organisation used the application Google Cloud print and then needed to replace it as Google discontinued it. Every stakeholder knew what Google Cloud print was or could at least work out for themselves that we were implementing new printing software.

If the name is not self-explanatory, i.e., the 'Virtual Park programme', then an explanatory 'What is the programme?' will be the first key message to develop. In this case, 'The Virtual Park programme is developing and implementing the ParkBook application for outdoor tennis court bookings' is an excellent example of a key message.

What, Why, Who, When, Where and How?

The best key messages are built on consensus using the well-rehearsed '5W's and How' framework. It's covered in many places, so I won't reproduce it here. I can't say that 100% of your key messages will fit this framework, but you will find that at least 90% of them will.

Examples of 5Ws and How

The following examples explore how key messages are developed using the '5Ws and How' for the Google Cloud Print project (Figure 1) and the Virtual Park programme (Figure 2). This should give you an idea of how to put this framework into practice.

What is the project?

We are installing the PrintRed application to replace Google Cloud Print.

Why is this being done?

Google is decommissioning Google Cloud Print, so it will no longer work.

Who is doing this, and who will use it?

The project team working with someone from each building with printers, will install and test PrintRed. All users, who need to print, will use the newly installed PrintRed servers.

When is it being done?

The PrintRed application will be rolled out nationally, site by site, over three months (January to March).

Where is it being done?

The PrintRed application will be installed at all sites that have a printer.

How is it being done?

The project team, working with someone from each building with printers, will install and test Print Red. Once PrintRed passes testing at the site, the old Google Cloud Print will be removed.

Figure 1 Examples of key messages for the Google Cloud Print replacement project

What is the programme?

We are developing and implementing the ParkBook application for outdoor tennis court bookings.

Why is this being done?

To let tennis players book online instead of at the park keeper's office.

Who is doing this, and who will use it?

The developers will develop the ParkBook application. The programme team will implement it. The IT department will maintain it. The tennis players and the park keepers will use it.

When is it being done?

The ParkBook application will go live on April 1st.

Where is it being done?

The ParkBook application is online, and the tennis courts are in Old Oak Park.

How is it being done?

The tennis court details and booking slots will be set up in the ParkBook application. The ParkBook website will be advertised to tennis players. The park keepers will be trained how to administer it.

Figure 2 Examples of key messages for the Virtual Park programme

Blending

You will inevitably find the '5Ws and How' blend when developing and using key messages. For example, it's natural to say, 'We are implementing the ParkBook application to allow tennis players to book online' This is fine, but it is helpful to remember that it's a blend of What and Why.

How to develop effective key messages

To be effective, key messages should be based on consensus within the programme, written in clear and simple language and be approved for use.

Be based on consensus within the programme

Consensus is important to ensure that key messages are accurate and that there is buy-in from everyone on the programme team. Without consensus, you will find different people saying different things without any reference as to what is correct. Equally, some people may say nothing as they are unsure what to say.

The key to gaining consensus is involving the appropriate people to develop each message and ensuring that those people have a realistic expectation that they will need to consider others' views. Consensus often requires individuals to compromise and acknowledge that they are aiming for the best possible consensus at that time. E.g., two colleagues might disagree on which month a product will be ready to test, say January or March. An appropriate key message might then be that the product will be ready to test in Qtr. 1.

Written in clear and simple language

Using straightforward language is vital when developing and conveying key messages. This ensures the message is easily understood and eliminates the potential for confusion and misunderstandings. It helps to avoid words that can be misunderstood or open to different interpretations, as does steering clear of technical jargon that stakeholders may need to learn.

Clear and simple language takes time to develop, but once done it's efficient for both the communicator and stakeholder.

Approved for use

Key messages should be approved for use so that everyone is 100% confident using them. There should be no doubt, and people should not be making things up as they go along. Ideally, approval should be done on a routine and regular basis at the approver's convenience rather than urgently just before needed when the approver must stop what they are doing to approve.

I don't want to recommend a specific approval process as it's likely to work best if you follow a process led by the approver. Examples I have worked with include, adding 'approving key messages' as an agenda item to an existing meeting agenda (i.e., Programme Senior Leadership Team or weekly project meeting), booking a short weekly meeting with the approver, or having the approver commit to responding to emailed approval requests within an agreed time frame.

Programme vision

The programme vision is usually an excellent example of a key message. The programme team have usually taken the time to base it on a consensus and write it in clear and simple language, and because it is published, it is approved for use.

Publishing dates

Dates are one of the key insights that stakeholders want. It is the When in the 5Ws covered previously. Having been party to many detailed and sometimes long discussions about the pros and cons of what and when to share, I can summarise that it comes down to three basic options:

1. Wait until you have fully confirmed dates to share
2. Publish dates with a tbc caveat
3. Publish dates and then correct them if they prove to be wrong

That's it, choose option 1, 2 or 3 and move on!

Stakeholder pack

The stakeholder pack is a versatile tool for engaging with stakeholders and, once created and approved for use, can be used by anyone in the programme. The pack should be produced using a presentation program such as Microsoft PowerPoint, Google Slides or something similar, depending on the standard tools available within the programme and the intended audience.

The stakeholder pack works best when it is kept up to date with all the current key messages in one place, presented in clear and simple language in a visually engaging way. See Figure 3 for examples.

Creating the stakeholder pack can also help the process of developing the key messages themselves. One of the challenges when developing key messages (based on consensus, written in clear and simple language, and approved for use) is getting the support you need from programme colleagues. Collaborating on an early draft of the stakeholder pack allows programme colleagues to produce something tangible together. In my experience, this can deliver a better and quicker outcome than working on the key messages and stakeholder pack separately.

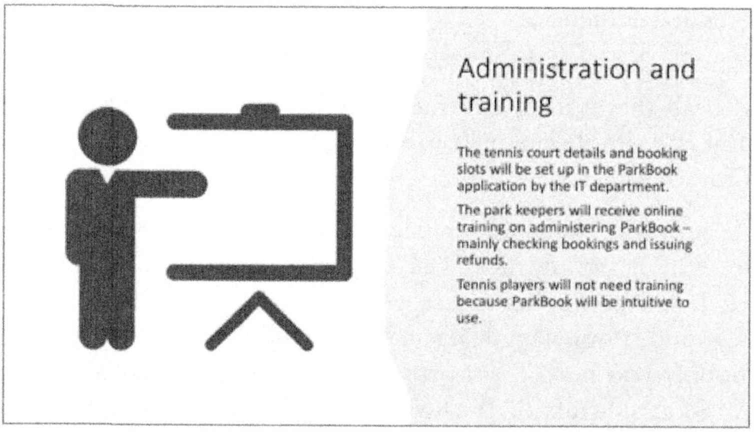

Figure 3 Two slides from the Virtual Park programme stakeholder pack presenting key messages in a visually engaging way

3

STEP 2 – MAPPING STAKEHOLDERS

At its most basic, a stakeholder map is a master list of the stakeholders and their contact details. It should only include stakeholders rather than members of the programme team. The Programme Management Office (PMO) or project manager usually holds contact details for team members.

Definition of a stakeholder

The first step is to agree on the definition of the term 'stakeholder'. This can vary to suit different programmes, but it is most often a derivative of 'stakeholders are people who have an interest in the programme, are particularly impacted by it themselves or represent groups of people who are impacted by it'.

There is a well-known statement 'Every customer/user is a stakeholder'. Whilst I recognise the value of this view in some contexts it's not a helpful perspective when developing a pragmatic approach to SE. Programmes have limited resources, and you need to prioritise the most important stakeholders.

Internal and external stakeholders

Some methodologies or programme professionals refer to internal and external stakeholders. I find this an inconsistent definition which can cause confusion. It is better to use the consistent definitions 'stakeholder' and 'programme team'.

What information do we need to capture?

Your stakeholder map can capture whatever information you feel is relevant. As a minimum, you should record the role, name, email address, tags, and the analysis you have undertaken (see stakeholder mapping approaches).

Recording both the name and role of the stakeholder is important as people are transient and roles are more stable. For example, when a finance manager (a common stakeholder for IT programmes) leaves their role, you will need to identify their replacement and engage with them. Whoever holds the role at the time, whether they are permanent, interim or 'just covering', is your stakeholder.

As digital communication is most prevalent now, email addresses tend to be the most important contact details to record. Not least because email is used to locate people on Teams, Google Meet and other collaboration tools. In other words, you will use an email address to find someone to message, call, or invite them to a meeting.

'Tags' are a generic name we give to the multiple extra characteristics, attributes, or contexts we might record for each stakeholder. Tags can also allow the grouping of stakeholders in a structured way. Examples of tags include what project(s) within a programme a particular stakeholder is engaged by and what (if any) programme boards they sit on.

Programme-wide stakeholder maps

There should be one programme-wide stakeholder map (master list). Whilst this is generally uncontroversial for standalone projects, it is more of a challenge for programmes made up of multiple projects. Individual projects and or project managers are often inclined to think it easier or more beneficial to maintain their own stakeholder maps rather than contribute to a programme-wide one. Two compelling reasons to have a programme-wide stakeholder map are to have a programme-wide perspective and a single master list of contacts.

A programme wide perspective

Getting a programme-wide perspective of stakeholders is very difficult unless you have a programme-wide stakeholder map. You would need to aggregate individual project stakeholder maps, which is very difficult due to the duplication of stakeholders across multiple projects, projects using different stakeholder mapping techniques or formats and people relying on their memory rather than writing a list. The benefits of a programme-wide perspective are:

- Programme management can see and manage the big picture. Examples include knowing how many stakeholders there are and identifying risks where some key stakeholders might become single points of failure.
- Stakeholder engagement roles can see and manage the big picture. This enables the most important stakeholders to be prioritised whilst ensuring all stakeholders are engaged, concentrating time and resources as effectively as possible.
- Project managers can see where their project stakeholders are also engaged elsewhere in the programme.

A single list of contact details

Contact details are essential for engaging with stakeholders via email, text, or phone. Without an accessible single list, you must ask individual project managers to pass on or cascade programme messages. This can mean some stakeholders will not receive anything, and others will receive the same message multiple times.

How to identify stakeholders

Any relevant research will highlight various techniques for identifying stakeholders. However, across these techniques, there are three common themes:

1. Everyone, or pragmatically almost everyone, in the programme team should contribute to identifying stakeholders.
2. Stakeholders themselves are vital to identifying stakeholders.
3. Identifying stakeholders is a continuous process rather than something that can be done as a one-off.

Identification of stakeholders by the programme team

The chances are you will need to be flexible in how you work with the programme team to identify stakeholders, as you will need to fit in with the competing priorities your programme colleagues are juggling. Occasionally you may work with the whole programme team simultaneously and with no stakeholders already mapped. In that case, there is a specific 'rapid listing' approach you can use that I cover in the last thoughts chapter. In my experience, this opportunity rarely arises, so we need to be pragmatic and get on with it as best we can. The key is just to get started spending time with programme colleagues and mapping stakeholders.

When planning stakeholder mapping sessions with programme colleagues, you will need to take into account some considerations. These considerations fall into three broad categories; Who can get together at one time? How do we work together? and What can we make use of? To some extent, these considerations interrelate.

Who can get together at one time?

Who from the programme team can you get together at one time? When you look at a programme organisation chart (or have it explained to you), you can see whether there are teams of people working together or individuals in roles. This is often a reflection of the scale of the programme. If there are teams of people, the preference would be to get the team together, but you may find it is pragmatic to talk to team members separately as individuals.

How do we work together?

Once a stakeholder mapping session is booked, how many people are in the session? If you have just one person, it's a conversation. If you have more than three, your challenges include keeping everyone engaged.

Is it in-person, virtual or hybrid? This is likely to be dictated by how colleagues in the programme already work together. You will be most successful if you defer to your colleagues' preferences. A stakeholder mapping session is unlikely to be the best time to try and introduce new interactive tools and new ways of working. Stakeholder mapping is a collaborative process, so the differences between in-person, virtual and hybrid sessions shine through. Virtual sessions are relatively easy to organise, but the way people work in the sessions varies a lot. Some people are used to working collaboratively with virtual whiteboards and shared documents etc., while others are only comfortable having conversations and listening to presentations. Often hybrid meetings can be the most challenging to run, although they are usually easier to organise than in-person meetings.

What can we make use of?

Is this the start of the stakeholder mapping process? i.e., are you starting with no prior stakeholder map and a blank sheet of paper or adding stakeholders to an existing stakeholder map? Sessions that add stakeholders to an existing stakeholder map usually start by reviewing the existing stakeholder map.

Over the programme's life, adding stakeholders to an existing stakeholder map is common.

Often, teams already have relevant lists of stakeholders they can bring to the table but may not realise it. Encouraging people to review existing lists is more effective than making people work on the spot or from memory. Relevant lists can include existing documentation and techniques like RACI or a circulation list of relevant sent emails.

Objectives of stakeholder mapping sessions

Although flexibility of approach is crucial, there are four standard objectives we want to prioritise in any stakeholder mapping session:

1. Everyone has a shared understanding of the definition of a stakeholder.
2. There is buy-in to the principle of a central stakeholder map.
3. There is a sense of collective ownership and involvement in the process.
4. The necessary analysis to map stakeholders is conducted using one of the approaches detailed later in Stakeholder mapping approaches.

Stakeholders can identify other stakeholders

Although stakeholders themselves have an essential role in identifying other stakeholders, there are two issues to be aware of.

First, how do you find the first stakeholders to identify other stakeholders?

Second, there is a risk that the first stakeholders you approach may perceive you as not having a grip on the programme if you must ask them who the stakeholders are!

With these issues in mind, I have found it effective to use a two-step process where the programme team first identifies all the stakeholders it can and then asks those stakeholders themselves to identify other potential stakeholders who still need to be added to the list. This is shown in Figure 4 as expanding circles where the programme team identifies some stakeholders, but only by asking those stakeholders can all stakeholders be identified.

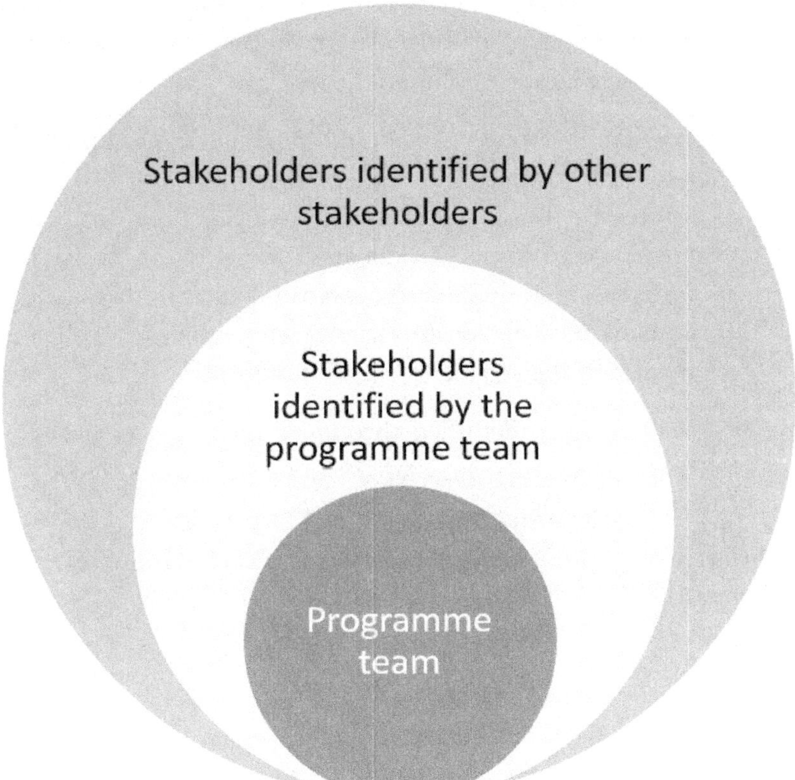

Figure 4 Expanding circles approach to identifying stakeholders

Stakeholders self-identifying

Stakeholders themselves initiate a lot of effective stakeholder engagement. Including the initial step of self-identification. It's essential to standardise how you respond to this as much as possible. The key points are:

- People are unlikely to say, "I want to be a stakeholder". They are more likely to show a specific interest in the programme, ask for a meeting or attempt to access some relevant documentation you may have previously shared with one of their colleagues.
- Programmes must validate the person's level of interest and relationship to the programme and respond appropriately. I generally advise that you embrace anyone who wants to be a stakeholder and only say no if necessary. Pragmatically you can default to them being considered a lower-importance stakeholder if you are unsure of their value to the programme.
- Stakeholders identified through this approach must be mapped like all other stakeholders.

Figure 5 shows that whilst stakeholders self-identify in different ways, the analysis, mapping, and onboarding can be standardised.

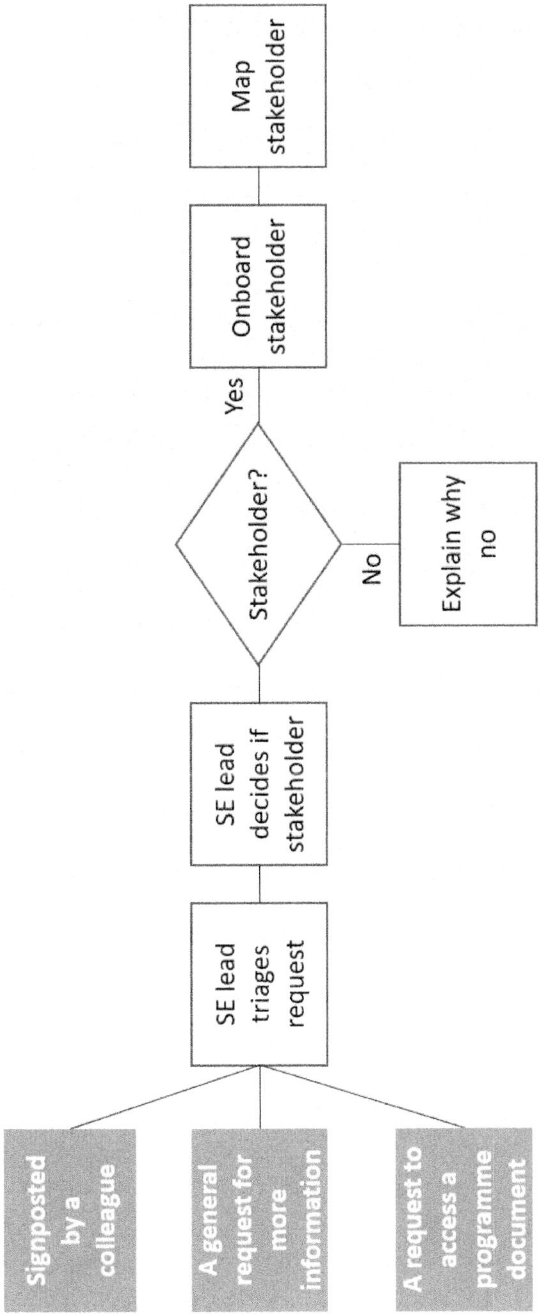

Figure 5 Stakeholders self-identifying as stakeholders

Large programmes have complex stakeholder maps

As programmes increase in size and complexity, stakeholder maps can become large and complex. This increases the work it takes to produce and maintain them. However, this is when they also become even more necessary.

One of the challenges is that colleagues sometimes need help comprehending the fundamental differences between delivering effective SE for small, relatively simple, and relatively fast projects versus large, complex programmes with more extended time frames.

In a small project, one person is often responsible for SE for the project's duration. In this case, it is realistic for one person to broadly remember the exact details that would be recorded on a stakeholder map, so the benefits of formally using one are less clear. In a programme, the scale and or complexity means; multiple people are involved in SE, there is far more detail to keep hold of, and often programme team members change over time. One person can't hold this information, so you must embed a trusted process to ensure consistency across everyone involved with SE and ease handover as the programme team changes over time.

The work must be done to realise the benefits detailed in the above section on programme-wide stakeholder maps. The only alternative is to fall back on individual projects doing their own stakeholder mapping, which is considerably less efficient.

Stakeholder mapping approaches

When mapping stakeholders, it is also necessary to analyse and segment them so you can better plan and carry out SE. You can find many ways to analyse stakeholders depending on your focus. In this guide, I briefly describe three of the most popular that are used in IT, technology and digital programmes. The power and interest grid (Figure 6), The influence and impact grid (Figure 7) and the stakeholder radar (Figure 8) as these three are the most well-known.

Unfortunately, despite some research, I have been unable to reliably identify the originators of any of these stakeholder mapping approaches, so I can't give any specific credit. Also, the naming convention for each is not 100% reliable. You can find examples of the stakeholder radar being used as a generic name to cover various other stakeholder mapping techniques. In this guide, I will only use the term stakeholder radar to describe the stakeholder radar itself (Figure 8).

The power and interest grid

The power and interest grid records stakeholders' power and interest in the programme. Two attributes, high or low interest and high or low power, combine to create four quadrants onto which stakeholders are mapped.

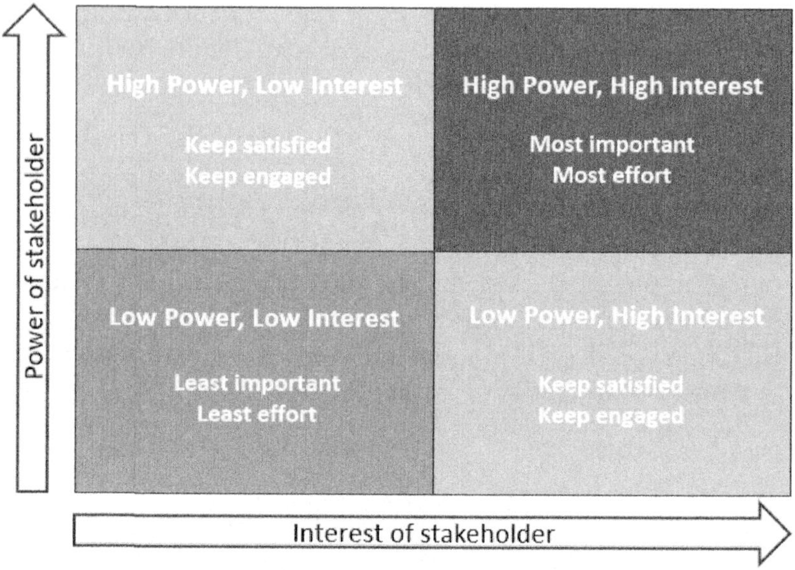

Figure 6 Power and interest grid for stakeholder mapping

The stakeholders with high power and high interest in the programme are the most important.

Next, some stakeholders have high power yet a low level of interest and low power but a high level of interest. Both these groups must be kept satisfied and engaged in the programme so they can help when needed. Low power and low interest stakeholders should have the least effort directed towards them.

The influence and impact grid

The influence and impact grid is similar to the power and interest grid, with two attributes rated high or low, resulting in four quadrants onto which stakeholders are mapped. Stakeholders are mapped on their influence (involvement) and the impact (the person's ability to affect changes) on the programme's planning and execution.

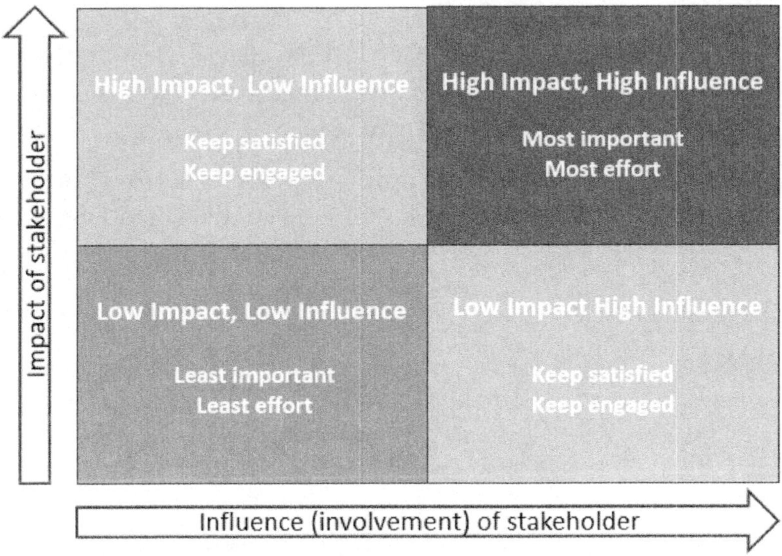

Figure 7 Influence and impact grid for stakeholder mapping

The most important stakeholders have the highest influence and impact on the programme.

Next, some stakeholders have a high level of influence yet a lower level of impact and a low level of influence but a substantially higher degree of impact. Both these groups must be kept satisfied and engaged in the programme so they can help when needed. Low influence and impact stakeholders should have the least effort directed towards them.

The stakeholder radar

In contrast to the previous mapping techniques, the stakeholder radar maps two attributes. The first attribute describes the level of engagement; vital, necessary, good, and courtesy. The names here are self-explanatory, with the most important stakeholders described as vital to engage. The second attribute describes the stakeholder's domain; customer, governance, provider, and influencer. The stakeholder domain describes the relationship between the stakeholder and the programme. This relationship often dictates the kind of insights and key messages the stakeholder will be most interested in and the role they may take.

Each attribute having four options results in a 16-sector grid that is shown as something resembling a radar (Figure 8).

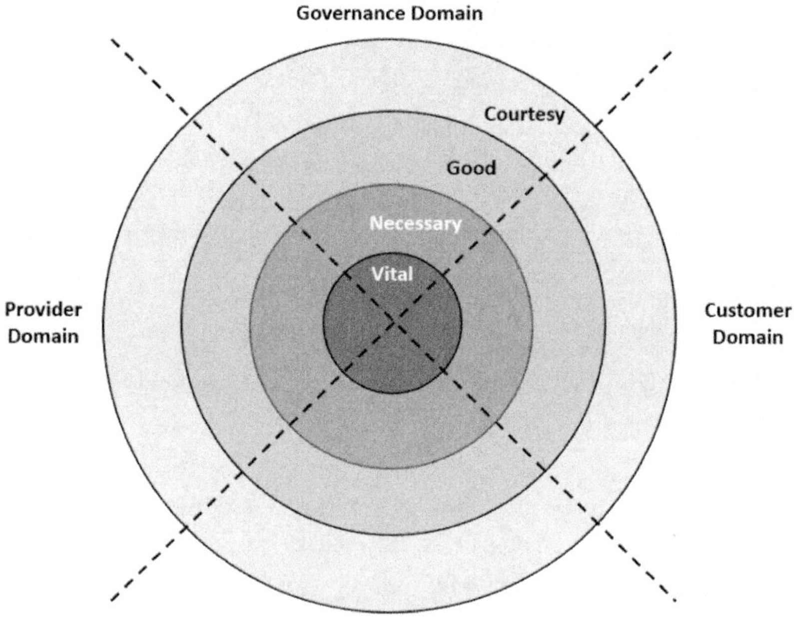

Figure 8 Stakeholder radar for stakeholder mapping

Common themes in stakeholder mapping

The power and interest grid, the influence and impact grid and the stakeholder radar notably have two common themes.

First, they identify the most important or useful stakeholders so you can prioritise them over the others. Prioritising stakeholders is essential as, pragmatically, you cannot treat all stakeholders as equally important.

Second, they are great visually, as stakeholders can be mapped directly onto their relative quadrants or sectors. This visual appeal is helpful; as mentioned before, we want colleagues to buy into the principle of a central stakeholder map and foster a sense of collective ownership and involvement in the stakeholder mapping process. A picture is worth a thousand words or an Excel spreadsheet!

The stakeholder radar in use in IT, technology and digital programmes

I prefer using the stakeholder radar for IT, technology and digital programmes. In addition to the two themes it has in common with the power and interest grid and the influence and impact grid, it also analyses the stakeholder's relationship with the programme. Analysing and recording this extra information is helpful while not affecting the ease of use. The extra information is helpful for four reasons.

1. The nature of a stakeholder's relationship with the programme usually dictates the kind of insights and key messages the stakeholder will be most interested in.
2. The nature of a stakeholder's relationship with the programme helps everyone understand the role the stakeholder has and, in turn, what help they might be able to offer the programme.

3. The increase to sixteen sectors allows more precise engagement targeting stakeholders with minimal extra effort. Engagement is most effective when it is tailored to specific audiences.

4. It can reflect how an individual stakeholder's relationship with the programme can change throughout its lifecycle. For example, the arrows in Figure 9 show how the mapping for the head of operations might change through the programme lifecycle when implementing a new CRM system for a sales team. First, they start as an influencer; through the procurement phase they have a governance role (signing off a purchase decision), and then once deployment starts, they move to be a customer. Other roles, such as chief executive, remain in the governance domain for the duration of the programme.

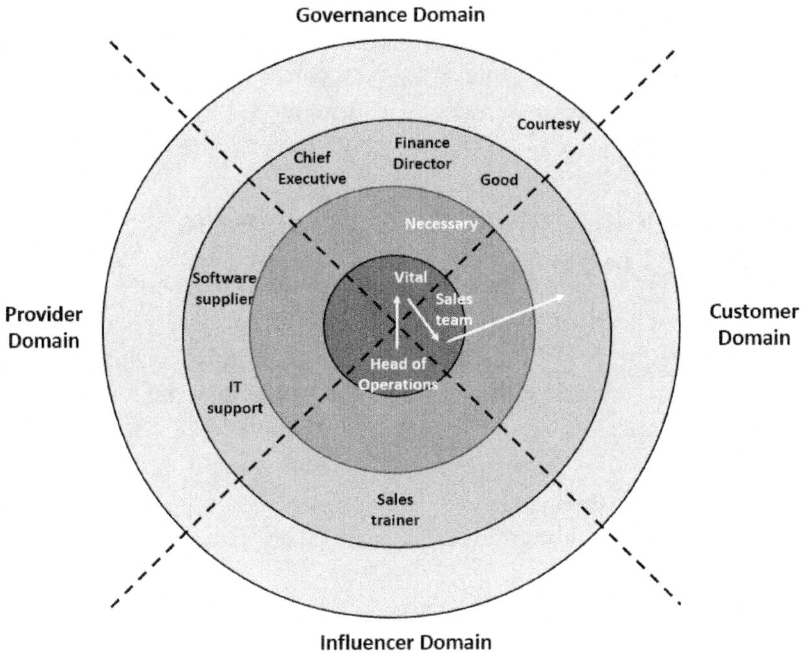

Figure 9 How a stakeholder's relationship with a programme can change over time

One concern raised about the stakeholder radar, also true of other approaches, is that it doesn't encourage a detailed enough analysis of stakeholders. This should be seen as a benefit, as a more detailed analysis may need the addition of sensitive and confidential information. As the stakeholder radar does not record this level of detail, it can be shared without limitations, enabling the programme and stakeholders to discuss nuances of individual stakeholders.

Stakeholder radar definitions

Definitions agreed across the programme encourage consistency. Whilst the terms used to describe the stakeholder radar's domain (influencer, governance, customer, provider)

and levels of engagement (vital, necessary, good, courtesy) are self-explanatory, each programme should formally agree on their own baseline definitions of those terms to match the specific considerations of the programme. Still, starting from scratch is unnecessary as the following are common baseline definitions that can be used:

Stakeholder radar domain baseline definitions

The stakeholder domain describes the relationship between the stakeholder and the programme. This relationship usually dictates the kind of insights and key messages the stakeholder will be most interested in, the role they are likely to have and what help they can provide. The following sections suggest some baseline definitions, some guidance on what kinds of insight they will be interested in and what role they are likely to have:

Governance

These stakeholders contribute to programme decision-making. They are most likely interested in insights and key messages that help them perform their role in setting strategic direction and goals, key decision-making, managing risk, monitoring performance, and providing oversight.

Influencers

These stakeholders can affect what the programme delivers. They are often subject matter experts or expert and experienced advisors. As their role is to share this expertise and perspective with the programme on behalf of the customers it is helpful if they have credibility with the customers and end users.

Their influence can cover programme design, desired outcomes, implementation and messaging.

Customers

These stakeholders represent end users or people who will use what the programme delivers, i.e., infrastructure. Their role is to provide valuable insights into the challenges, needs and expectations of the intended users. Their involvement is essential for designing and delivering programmes that effectively meet user needs, drive user adoption, and achieve desired outcomes.

Some customer stakeholders can also play a vital role in testing and validating programme deliverables. They can provide feedback on prototypes, pilot projects, or beta versions, helping identify issues, bugs, or areas for improvement.

Providers

These stakeholders are suppliers of the software and services required by the programme. Their role is to contribute essential resources, expertise, and support. Providers often possess specialised expertise and knowledge in their respective fields. They bring technical skills, industry insights, and best practices to the programme, contributing to its design, implementation, and operational efficiency.

They can also have a role in ensuring quality assurance and compliance with relevant standards and regulations.

Stakeholder radar level of engagement baseline definitions

The level of engagement records the stakeholder's relative importance to the programme. The levels are vital, necessary, good and courtesy, with vital clearly being the most important. Much like other mapping approaches, categorising the level of importance helps move the programme beyond seeing every stakeholder as essential.

A stakeholder's relative importance to the programme often differs from their seniority in an organisation. Commonly vital stakeholders are not the most senior people in an organisation but those lower down tasked with supporting the programme. The most senior stakeholders often don't have the time to invest in individual programmes, so they will delegate that responsibility to someone more junior.

The following baseline definitions for the levels of importance should be seen as a starting point. They do not dictate how often or how stakeholders should be engaged. To promote consistency, that is something that large programmes must decide for themselves.

Vital to engage

Vital to engage stakeholders are those who must be engaged proactively and regularly through the life of the programme to make day-to-day and weekly progress. Engagement with these stakeholders is likely to be the most frequent unless directed by the stakeholders themselves.

These stakeholders will almost certainly be involved in key decision points either directly or indirectly through colleagues or programme governance processes.

Programme representatives should build rapport and trust with these stakeholders so that they feel comfortable contacting each other anytime they wish to ask for help, raise concerns, etc.

Necessary to engage

Necessary to engage stakeholders need proactive engagement but on a less regular basis than vital to engage stakeholders.

These stakeholders are likely to be involved at key decision points rather than on a day-to-day or even weekly basis.

Again, programme representatives should build rapport and trust with stakeholders so that they feel comfortable contacting each other anytime to ask for help, raise concerns etc.

A typical example of a necessary to engage stakeholder is the head of a department or director who has delegated regular engagement to one of their team members. They are not directly involved week to week but will ultimately have to sign off key decisions. In this example, the delegated team member would be the vital stakeholder, and their senior would be the necessary stakeholder.

Good to have engaged

These stakeholders are unlikely to be engaged proactively and regularly but should still be fully aware of the programme.

These stakeholders may have some indirect influence through vital to engage and necessary to engage stakeholders but will not be directly involved in key decision points. They should be considered vital or necessary if they are directly involved in key decision points.

Programme representatives and stakeholders in this category should know who each other are, so they can contact each other if or when necessary.

Courtesy to inform

These stakeholders need the lowest level of engagement. This may be the default level for stakeholders who have self-identified but are not seen as requiring a higher level of engagement as they have no importance to the programme.

The stakeholder and programme representative should have each other's contact details on file but would not usually make contact proactively or regularly.

The stakeholder radar evolves through the life of the programme

Stakeholders will change over the life of any programme. Reasons for change may be due to them leaving roles or moving domains, i.e., an influencer can move to governance or customer (Figure 9).

Stakeholders changing domains often reflect the stage the programme is at. E.g., there are likely to be more influencer stakeholders during the build phase of a programme. In contrast, there are likely to be more customer stakeholders during the programme's delivery or rollout phase. This means it's a good idea to schedule an in-depth review and update of the stakeholder radar when the programme transitions from one phase to another. This review could be scheduled as part of the programme's routine tasks planned as part of the transition from one phase to another.

The stakeholder radar should always reflect the programme

It's important that the stakeholder radar reflects the current picture rather than the past or future. The stakeholder map should be like holding up a mirror to the programme at that moment in time. The biggest changes are most likely to occur between programme phases.

Resolving common stakeholder radar issues

Due to the nature of a programme-wide stakeholder map, there will inevitably be times when disagreements arise, and stakeholders appear to occupy more than one level of engagement or stakeholder domain. Whilst it is tempting to think this extra complexity should be recorded on the stakeholder radar, this should be resisted as there is no tangible benefit to this.

When stakeholders appear to occupy more than one level of engagement and or more than one stakeholder domain, it usually comes down to one of three things that can be easily resolved.

More than one level of engagement

If there is disagreement about which level of engagement the stakeholder should occupy, this is resolved by attributing to them the highest level of engagement. A stakeholder who is vital to engage for one project and courtesy to inform for another project is a vital to engage stakeholder for the whole programme.

More than one stakeholder domain

This is usually about timing and the phase of the programme. By design, the stakeholder radar can accommodate stakeholders moving from one domain to another over the life of the programme. An example of this is when a stakeholder might be seen as both an influencer and a customer. This would be recorded as influencer initially and then moved to customer when they are no longer influencing the programme. This is illustrated in Figure 9, where the domain of a head of operations stakeholder changes over the life of the programme.

Disagreement over the domain

The least common is when there is disagreement about what role a stakeholder has in the programme. i.e., a stakeholder might want to be involved in the governance of the programme (or a programme colleague may think they should be), but they are not currently part of programme governance. This is a disagreement about the stakeholder's actual role rather than how to record them on the stakeholder radar. Once there is consensus as to what the stakeholder's role is (are they to become part of the programme governance or not?) the stakeholder mapping then becomes easy.

Stakeholder engagement for secret programmes

Within IT, technology and digital, some programmes prefer to keep what they deliver a secret or, more likely, on a need-to-know basis. In my experience, examples include some cyber security programmes and developing commercially sensitive products.

Programmes that wish to be secret or on a need-to-know basis will take the approach of involving as few people as possible. Although it might seem counterintuitive, SE is still important and arguably more essential to a programme taking this approach. In the case of secret programmes, most techniques in this guide stay the same, but the mindset changes with respect to who is a stakeholder. and what key messages are appropriate for each stakeholder.

The biggest difference can be shown in Figure 10. Stakeholders should be carefully identified by the programme rather than more widely.

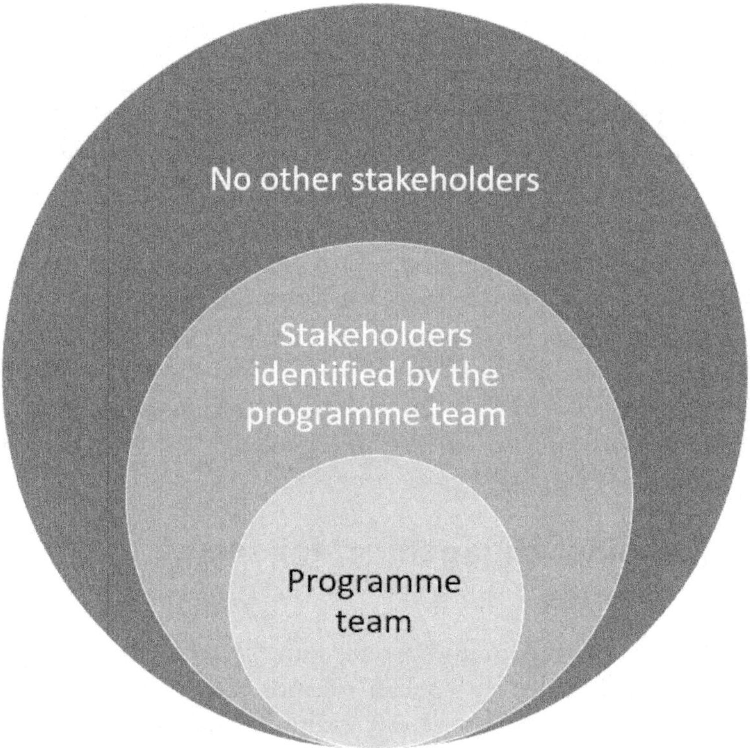

Figure 10 Secret programmes, restricted approach to identifying stakeholders

4

STEP 3 – ENGAGING WITH STAKEHOLDERS

Although this step is the easiest of the three, as you just need to start talking to stakeholders, in practice, it often seems the hardest. There are genuine concerns that you need to overcome. Stakeholders are busy people; you don't know them and might worry about how they will react and what you can share. This chapter covers how to approach and overcome your main concerns and ensure you have meaningful conversations with stakeholders.

Stakeholders never complain about over-engagement

One of the most common concerns is that you might over-engage with stakeholders or disturb them when they are busy. This concern is unfounded, and you must rise above it. The reasons stakeholders don't complain about over-engagement, in no particular order, are:

- They understand that effective engagement is essential for programme success and welcome the opportunity to contribute their input, maybe highlighting opportunities that would otherwise be missed. This is especially true of more senior or experienced stakeholders.

- Being engaged allows them to manage the level of engagement to suit themselves. You might experience this as them tuning out from what you are saying, limiting the conversation by telling you how long they have ('I only have 10 minutes') and signposting you to someone else. This can sometimes feel awkward, and it is important not to take it personally!
- As humans, the experience of being excluded, ignored, or undervalued is felt more strongly than that of being included unnecessarily.

What not to share

Another common concern is what can be shared and when. In my experience, it's easy for programme teams to spend lots of time and effort discussing, sometimes arguing, about what should or should not be shared with stakeholders. Again, many people are naturally inclined to refrain from proactively sharing information with stakeholders for various reasons. These reasons can vary from genuinely good reasons to positively negative ones. Some examples include worrying that something might need to be changed later, wanting to avoid having difficult conversations with stakeholders and people wanting to make themselves irreplaceable by gatekeeping knowledge.

To cut through these concerns, I advocate starting from a position of sharing everything with stakeholders, with three exceptions that I cover here. If you don't want to share something, the easiest place to start is to leave it out, or in other words, omit it. This works well until people ask you about it directly. But there is no need to worry or lie; you just need to be prepared with what to say.

Commercially sensitive or confidential

This one is arguably the most obvious. Undoubtedly, some information is commercially sensitive or confidential. If asked directly, you can say, 'I'm sorry, we can't share that information as it is confidential'.

Not yet the appropriate time

Some information might need to go through internal programme governance or be shown first to senior stakeholders for approval. If asked directly, you can say, 'We have made a proposal, but it needs to be formally approved before I can share it with you'.

Not clear what it means for stakeholders

Stakeholders are busy people. They don't want to be given every update as and when the programme receives it. They want added insight into what it means for them. They would prefer you to take the time to work it through and provide valuable insight. i.e., a supplier might provide an update that there will be a three-week delay. Rather than share this with the stakeholders immediately, take the time to work through the overall impact and what, if anything, can be done to mitigate it. If asked directly, you can share what you know and include a caveat. In the example given, you could say, 'The supplier has said there is a three-week delay, but we want to work through what that means before we share it with you'.

Meaningful conversations

Historically the basis of a meaningful conversation would be a verbal conversation in person, or on the phone. Now you might find yourself talking virtually on a video conferencing app, texting via chat or emailing. The ideas in this section can be applied to all methods of engagement.

We are all busy people, so when talking with stakeholders, it's essential to have meaningful conversations with them. We are looking for a sweet spot between inflexibly following a fixed agenda and thoughtlessly talking about whatever comes to mind. Having meaningful conversations allows you to efficiently use everyone's time, develop rapport and build trust.

A lot has been written about meaningful conversations from a psychological perspective. Focusing on a professional, rather than personal, perspective can be summarised as; engagement should be purposeful, and that purpose should be clear to all. Don't worry if you feel like you don't have much to say. Just have a shorter meeting.

How do we find that sweet spot? Well, personally, after a few minutes of small talk, I like to cover some of the following areas, according to what's important at the time:

- Stakeholder validation – confirm if they are the right stakeholder. If they are, great! Do they know of anyone else we should be talking to as well? Can they help identify any additional stakeholders? If they are not the right person, can they signpost you to someone they think might be appropriate?

- Talk through programme key messages and share more detailed insights if they ask and you know the detail.

- Answer their questions – either immediate clarifications or, if you are uncertain, commit to finding out and letting them know within a specific time frame.

- Capture their feedback and relevant insights – there can be a slight overlap with answering questions here, but this area is broader and more about listening and recording what's relevant for you and the programme.

- Ask them to provide what the programme needs from them at an opportune time.

Unsurprisingly engaging stakeholders in meaningful conversations requires preparation in advance and follow-up as appropriate. Some of the above points may need to be covered occasionally whilst others might be repeated regularly.

Whilst not focusing overtly on rapport and trust building, following this technique will nonetheless do just that. Especially important for building trust is to do what you say you will do promptly. If you said you would get them the answer to that question, make sure you do so proactively. Invest in building rapport and trust in this way; then, at crucial moments, you can leverage the relationships you have built to help speed up decisions and provide support at critical times.

Go at the pace of the stakeholder

This principle originated in customer-centric organisations but is equally valid for SE. The key is recognising that each stakeholder has different preferences and needs. For example, a stakeholder might prefer high-level, fast-paced and a minimal number of engagements. At the other end of the scale, a stakeholder might prefer more in-depth, slower-paced, and more engagements. Remember that if we can meet stakeholders where they are, we will build stronger relationships which leads to better outcomes.

If you feel you have little to share, it is still a great time to listen

There is often a stage when the programme feels it is too early to share with stakeholders, as there is very little to share. Don't let these concerns stop you. We still need to understand a lot: stakeholders' needs, challenges, the language/ jargon they use and their perceptions, etc. I like to keep a quote top of mind.

"If I were to summarize in one sentence the single most important principle I have learned in the field of interpersonal relations, it would be this: Seek first to understand, then to be understood."

Dr Stephen R. Covey

A balanced stakeholder engagement plan

Stakeholders and programme colleagues often hold their own views on the best engagement methods, usually based on their own preferences and biases. But appreciating the equal importance of all engagement methods is preferable because, for every pro, there is also a corresponding con. For instance, regular 1-2-1 in-person meetings are often perceived as the gold standard, but they can also be an inefficient use of programme time. On the other hand, responding to stakeholders or potential stakeholders who contact the programme is often an efficient and effective use of programme resources. However, it can be perceived negatively (as too passive) by stakeholders and programme colleagues alike. Setting up and maintaining a programme website can be very effective for reaching large audiences, but it's unlikely to be an efficient use of resources if the programme is only of short duration.

Planning for a balance of engagement methods is therefore essential if you don't want to end up over-focusing on one area at the expense of another, i.e. if you spend all your time travelling and giving presentations to large groups, you might not be available to have that urgent 1-2-1 meeting with a vital stakeholder concerned about an issue.

Once you have mapped your stakeholders and identified the most important ones, planning your engagements will allow you to focus time-intensive 1-2-1 meetings on key stakeholders whilst using efficient large-scale methods to keep the less important stakeholders informed.

Types, methods and ways of engaging with stakeholders

There are many ways of engaging with stakeholders, and for the best outcomes, the programme needs to embrace most of them (if not all). A non-exhaustive list of SE methods includes:

- Meetings
- Training sessions
- Workshops
- Test sessions
- Presentations
- Website updates
- Posters
- Email newsletters
- Answering questions from stakeholders
- Information stalls
- Adverts

Determining how, when, where and with whom to engage can be nuanced and complex. Deciding which engagement methods will be used with which stakeholders is essential for a clear and effective plan to take shape.

Planning stakeholder engagement methods in more detail

To plan a pragmatic approach to SE, it helps to look at engagement methods in more depth. In my experience, each engagement method from the list above consists of ten possible considerations grouped into four groups (Figure 11). These groups are: 1. Initiation (proactive v responsive engagement), 2. Scale (1-2-1 or 1-2-2 meeting v small group v large scale), 3. Format (in-person v virtual v hybrid) and 4. Regularity (regular v ad hoc).

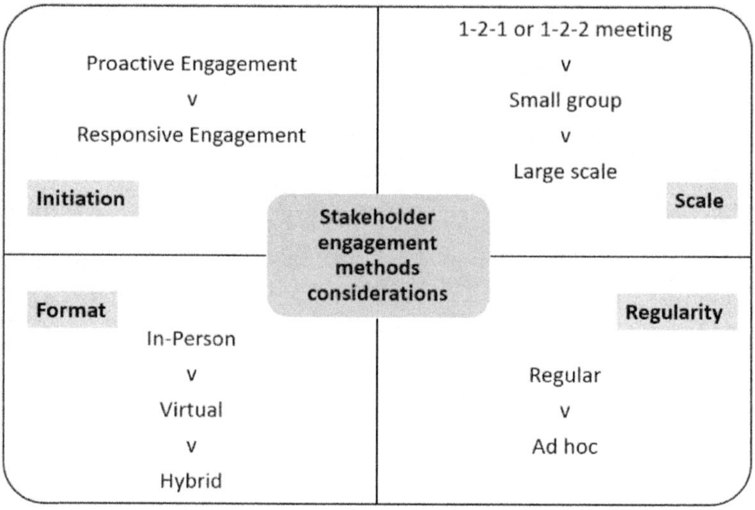

Figure 11 Engagement methods, 4 groups of considerations

The optimal blend of engagement methods is likely to change in response to the duration, scale, and phase of the programme, as well as the specific characteristics of the organisation that the programme is delivering to.

Thinking consistently in terms of these four groups of considerations can help inform planning SE throughout the programme lifecycle.

Example 1

Engaging with a vital governance stakeholder, through all phases of the programme (proactive engagement, 1-2-1 meeting, in-person, regular).

Example 2

Producing an information poster for necessary customer stakeholders during the roll-out phase of the programme (proactive engagement, large scale, in-person and virtual, ad-hoc).

Example 3

Presenting to a team of good to have engaged customers who ask about the programme (responsive engagement, small group, hybrid, ad hoc)

See the case study (Chapter 7) for more examples of this.

Delivering efficient stakeholder engagement

The stakeholder pack is the most useful tool for most engagement methods. No more reinventing the wheel.

- It's great for initial meetings with people, and it can be helpful to refer to at later meetings.
- It's ideal for giving those stakeholders attending training sessions, workshops and test sessions an insight into the programme.
- By design, it's ideal for presentations and information stalls.
- It will reduce the differences between proactive and responsive engagement as you will use the same preapproved key messages with both.
- It will allow you to be consistent whether you are talking to someone on the phone or designing a poster to be displayed.

Be prepared to repeat yourself

It's necessary to develop a mindset that repeating yourself is ok and is, in fact, a good thing. It might feel like an ineffective way to spend your time, but being prepared to repeat yourself is key to engaging effectively with stakeholders.

First, you have no choice, logistically you will share the same key messages with different stakeholders at different times at different locations. New stakeholders will constantly be identified as programmes evolve and stakeholders themselves move on to different roles and are replaced. Also, some stakeholders will tell you that they have not been told even though you know they have.

Second, good communicators embrace repetition as a technique to make sure people understand and remember what they are saying. It is like saying these programme key messages are important, and I want to make sure you get them. Additionally, repeating yourself to the same stakeholders gives them a second chance to understand and remember the key messages.

Finally, if you still need convincing, look at how often politicians repeat the same speech or at least use the same slogans and talking points. Establishing a consistent narrative by emphasising key messages is a common strategy.

5

LAST THOUGHTS

The three-step process works best as a cycle

This guide is written as a three-step sequential process to make step 3, the actual engagement with stakeholders as effective as possible. However, you will find that some aspects of step 2 and step 3 could influence the earlier steps. Examples of this include:

- When engaging with stakeholders, they may ask additional questions. Some of these will require the development of additional key messages.
- When engaging with stakeholders, some will signpost you to additional stakeholders that you will want to map and in turn engage with.
- When mapping stakeholders, you might identify stakeholders that will be interested in specific key messages that you have not yet developed,

When this happens, there is a temptation to go back and forth to earlier steps trying to improve the key messages and the stakeholder mapping. The risk with this is you lose the focus on the objective of engaging with stakeholders effectively. A better way to approach it is as a cycle so that you can keep moving forward see Figure 12

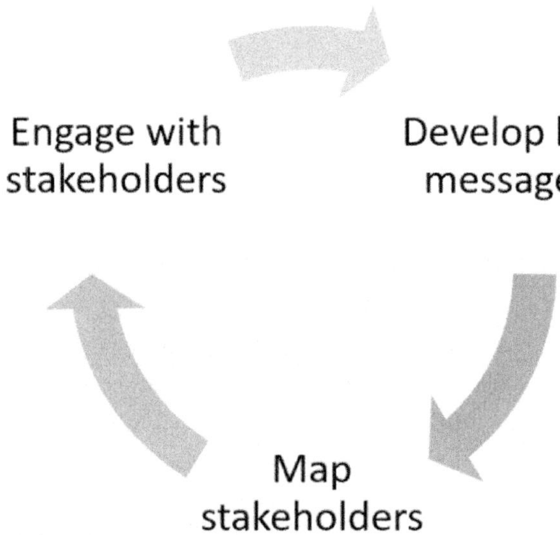

Figure 12 The three-step process seen as a cycle

Developing a stakeholder engagement strategy

If you want to develop a SE strategy for an IT, technology or digital programme this three-step process can form the cornerstone of it. You also need to make sure your strategy aligns with the programme and corporate objectives, so you may need to do some tweaking. A good example of tweaking to meet programme objectives is the earlier section on SE for secret programmes.

Personally, I think it's worth developing a SE strategy and getting it formally approved for all but the very smallest projects. Doing so will bring well-rehearsed benefits, which are: ensuring alignment with programme and corporate objectives, maximising resources, managing risks and fostering alignment and coordination within the programme.

The last of these, fostering alignment and coordination within the programme, is especially important for SE as it directly helps with one of the challenges for SE professionals, getting buy-in from colleagues and support to develop key messages and map stakeholders.

Onboarding stakeholders

Onboarding stakeholders is a standardised process that familiarises them with the programme. Within SE, it is also shorthand for confirming that the stakeholder has also been analysed and recorded on the stakeholder map. The goal of onboarding is that you and your programme colleagues can be confident that all stakeholders recorded on the stakeholder map have a baseline shared understanding that can be relied upon and built on as appropriate. At the end of the onboarding process, the stakeholder should; be aware of the project, workstream or workshop they are a stakeholder for and how it fits into the programme, have all relevant key messages regarding this shared with them, and be aware of who their programme contact is in case they have any questions or concerns.

Onboarding should be completed as quickly as possible but as always, the timescale may be dictated by the stakeholder. Sometimes due to the onboarding process extending over a few days, it's not clear on the stakeholder map if a recently added stakeholder has been fully onboarded or not. In my experience, it is not worth being overly concerned about this as the likelihood of it being an issue is low and the impact is low. Also, in mitigation, if the stakeholder is mid-way through the process with one person and another person approaches them it's very likely they will join the two conversations up for you by saying something along the lines of 'yes, your colleague has already talked to me and I am meeting them next week to discuss in more detail'.

6

TECHNIQUES FROM THIS GUIDE

Rapid listing for the whole programme team

Rapid listing, or a form of it, is an ideal technique for stakeholder mapping when you get the opportunity to work with a large group and no stakeholder mapping has been done yet. In my experience, this opportunity seldom arises, but some of these ideas can also be used in other contexts.

Rapid listing is a technique used to generate many ideas quickly. It involves making a list of as many ideas as possible in a short amount of time. It encourages a flow of ideas without self-censorship or judgment. It can also generate a sense of collective ownership and involvement in the process.

In brief, the aim is to have everyone in the group contribute to one combined list of stakeholders. We use a structured, step-by-step approach to keep it as open as possible for as long as possible. We try to avoid the group work issue where we often capture the contributions of outspoken individuals whilst quieter members keep themselves to themselves and end up contributing little and not feeling part of the process.

We start with individuals creating their own lists, then an intermediate step where we join people into small groups and combine lists. We then go around the groups to create one combined list. Finally, we can focus on the analysis and recording necessary to complete a stakeholder map as a group.

The step-by-step process in more detail is as follows:

1. Brief the group on the process. The brief, in this case, has three parts.

- Sharing the programme's agreed definition of a stakeholder
- Sharing an insight into the attributes of the stakeholder radar
- Housekeeping as to how this is being done practically. This will vary depending on the forum. In person, you can share printouts and or put posters on the walls, and people can handwrite lists and post-it notes. If the session is virtual, you will need to use virtual tools that people are used to using, e.g. Teams Whiteboard, Miro, Jamboard, Mentimeter, and Virtual Chat. There are no tools that are noticeably better than others. It is more important to use the tools people are used to.

2. Each person has 10 minutes to make their own list of stakeholders. Encourage people to generate a list of stakeholders as long as possible without analysing them or worrying about their importance. We are looking for many examples rather than considering who is the most important and how relevant they are.

3. Once everyone has their own list, we need to group people into small groups to compile joint lists. This is an intermediate step, and the size of these groups is not particularly significant but should consider the group's overall size. Each group should contain at least one person who is confident to speak for the group. The joint list should be a combination of each individual list without any consideration given to analysing the stakeholders.
4. Creating one list should now be carried out where each group shares one of the stakeholders from their list without repeating any already shared by another group. As we go around from group to group, each group should add one stakeholder to the central list and cross off those whom other groups have volunteered. We keep going around until each group has shared its stakeholders without repeating others. Once groups reach the end of their lists, individuals should be encouraged to add stakeholders they may have just thought of.
5. The final step is to assess and record the stakeholders on the stakeholder map.

The stakeholder radar recorded using Microsoft Lists

There are benefits to using a modern tool such as Microsoft Lists to capture the information you wish to hold on your stakeholder radar.

First, stakeholders often have multiple and overlapping characteristics, attributes, and contexts, which evolve over time. With a modern tool, you can record these as tags in a multichoice field rather than add multiple additional fields, as you would with spreadsheets. You can also add additional tags in the future as and when needed.

Second, Microsoft Lists reduces user errors by separating the storing of data and the viewing of data, tracking all changes, and providing versioning of changes (which allows rollback).

Finally, you can automate tasks such as identifying which stakeholders are due a review and integration into email.

Figure 13 shows an example of a stakeholder radar being recorded in Microsoft Lists.

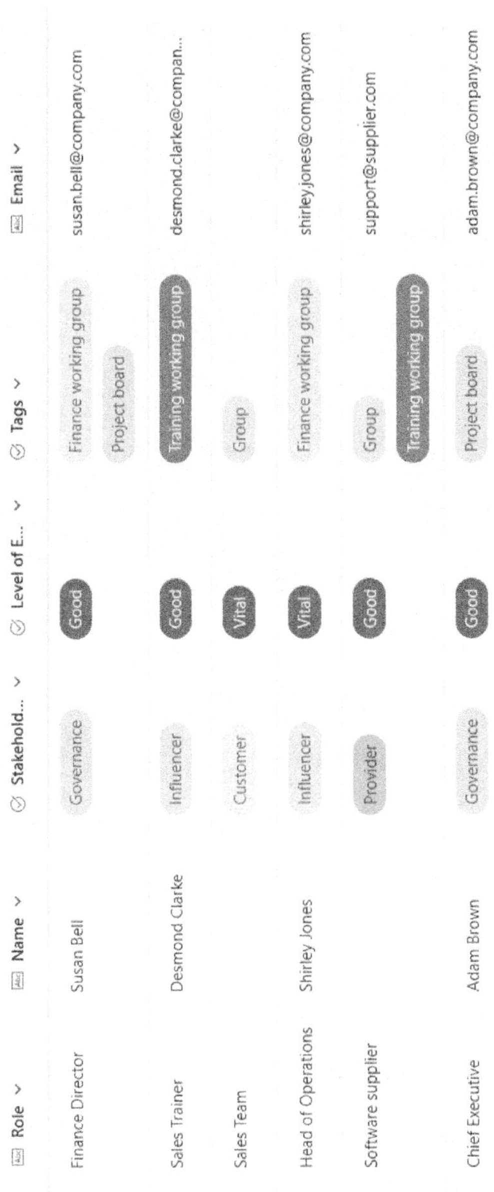

Role	Name	Stakehold...	Level of E...	Tags	Email
Finance Director	Susan Bell	Governance	Good	Finance working group, Project board	susan.bell@company.com
Sales Trainer	Desmond Clarke	Influencer	Good	Training working group	desmond.clarke@compan...
Sales Team		Customer	Vital	Group	
Head of Operations	Shirley Jones	Influencer	Vital	Finance working group	shirley.jones@company.com
Software supplier		Provider	Good	Group, Training working group	support@supplier.com
Chief Executive	Adam Brown	Governance	Good	Project board	adam.brown@company.com

Figure 13 Screenshot of a stakeholder radar using Microsoft Lists

7

CASE STUDY

This case study is an opportunity to look at the three-step process using a practical example. The scenario is the Virtual Park programme. This programme brought online bookings for public tennis courts to a park run by a social enterprise on behalf of the local council. The park and tennis courts are imaginary but based on real examples. The programme had three phases, development, implementation and go live.

Step 1 - Developing key messages

These key messages have already been shown in Figure 2, but they are repeated here for ease.

What is the programme?

We are developing and implementing the ParkBook application for outdoor tennis court bookings.

Why is this being done?

To let tennis players book online instead of at the park keeper's office.

Who is doing this, and who will use it?

The developers will develop the ParkBook application. The programme team will implement it. The IT department will maintain it. The tennis players and the park keepers will use it.

When is it being done?

The ParkBook application will go live on April 1st.

Where is it being done?

The ParkBook application is online, and the tennis courts are in Old Oak Park.

How is it being done?

The tennis court details and booking slots will be set up in the ParkBook application. The ParkBook website will be advertised to tennis players. The park keepers will be trained how to administer it.

Simultaneously, a stakeholder pack of 5 slides was produced to support engagement with stakeholders. It presented the key messages in a visually engaging and easy-to-use presentation.

Step 1 - Stakeholder pack - slides 1 & 2

Step 1 - Stakeholder pack - slides 3 & 4

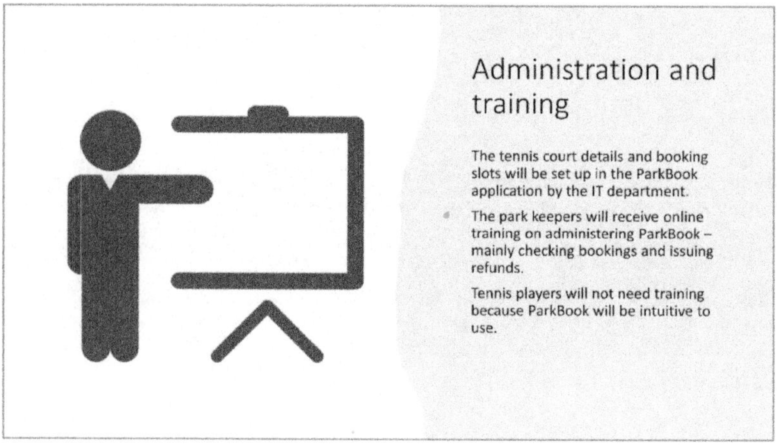

Step 1 - Stakeholder pack - slide 5

Step 2 - Mapping stakeholders

Step two is mapping stakeholders using a stakeholder radar. You can see how most stakeholders don't remain static. The park manager and park keepers started as influencers during the development phase but moved to the governance and customers domains, respectively, during the implementation and go live phases. The tennis club and tennis players started as good to engage during the development and implementation stage but became more important as the programme moved towards go live.

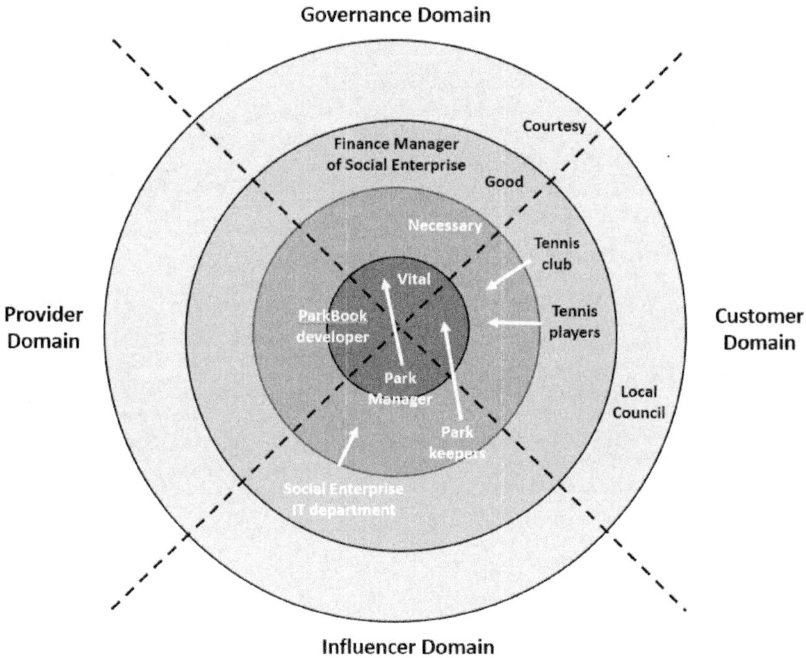

Step 3 - Engaging with stakeholders

The stakeholder engagement plan included a variety of types, methods and ways of engaging with stakeholders:

- Meetings with the head park keeper during the development phase (proactive engagement, 1-2-1)
- Training sessions for park keepers during the implementation phase (proactive engagement, small group)
- Meetings with the finance manager during all phases (proactive engagement, 1-2-1, regular)
- Meetings with the park manager during all phases (proactive engagement, 1-2-1, regular)
- Meetings with the developers during all phases (proactive engagement, 1-2-1)
- Meetings with the IT team during all phases (proactive, 1-2-1, regular)
- Meetings with the tennis club committee during all phases (proactive engagement, small group, ad-hoc)
- Website update on the park website for the tennis players during go live (proactive engagement, large scale, virtual, ad-hoc)
- Test sessions with selected tennis players during test phase (proactive engagement, 1-2-1, ad hoc)
- Posters at the tennis courts for tennis players during go live phase (proactive, large scale)
- Responsive ad-hoc engagement as required during all phases (responsive, ad-hoc)

Looking at the plan in detail, you will note three things. First, not all considerations are relevant in all cases. There is often a degree of flexibility available. For example, when planning the SE, meetings with the head park keeper could have been virtual or in-person (format), ad hoc or regular (regularity). You might want to record the format and the regularity once it has become clear or has happened, but it is unnecessary to dictate it.

Second, it becomes clear that the stakeholder pack could be directly used for the majority (8 out of 11) of the planned stakeholder engagement methods.

Finally, the key messages could be used in the other three engagement methods.

LIST OF PICTURES IN THIS BOOK

ABOUT THE AUTHOR

Andrew Powney has been a stakeholder engagement specialist in IT, technology, and digital programmes and projects since 2016. In this guide, Andrew distils his years of research and expertise into a pragmatic three-step guide that any project manager, change manager, or stakeholder engagement professional can use.

Printed in Great Britain
by Amazon

55058315R00050